Contents

Acknowledgements

We would like to thank members of the King's Fund Working Group on Age Discrimination who encouraged us to carry out this survey and gave us valuable advice and feedback.

Above all, thanks must go to the senior managers who participated in this survey and who made time in their busy schedules to share with us their reflections on age discrimination in local health and social care services. We are most grateful to them for their honesty and openness.

Emilie Roberts, Janice Robertson and Linda Seymour

Executive summary

Background

Between May and September 2001, the King's Fund carried out a telephone survey of 100 senior managers working in health and social services in England. The aims of the survey were:

- to find out how much they believed age discrimination was affecting services in their local area
- to discover what they were doing to combat it.

The survey took place following publication of the *National Service Framework (NSF) for Older People* in March 2001. In the *NSF for Older People*, the Government had indicated its determination to 'root out age discrimination' in health and social care, and had directed NHS organisations and local authorities with social services responsibilities to tackle the problem over the coming year.

The survey was conducted with senior managers who have the responsibility for putting the *NSF for Older People* into action, including:

- chief executives from primary care trusts and NHS community trusts
- medical directors from acute and specialist trusts
- directors of social services.

A total of 75 managers took part in the survey, a response rate of 75 per cent, representing a spread of experience in a diverse range of NHS trusts and social services departments across England.

Key findings

Presence of age discrimination

- Three out of four senior managers believed that age discrimination existed in some form or other in services in their local area.
- Many believed that ageism was endemic.
- Some gave examples of discrimination that they felt were justified or favoured older people.
- Only around a quarter of respondents felt there was little or no age discrimination within local services.

Type of age discrimination

- Most of the examples of age discrimination described by senior managers in their services constituted direct discrimination, i.e. policies restricting access to particular units, facilities and treatments by setting upper or lower age limits.

- Far fewer instances of indirect discrimination were described.
- This does not mean, of course, that age-related policies are more prevalent than other forms of discrimination. They may merely be more visible and easily identifiable – especially at a time when managers were being directed to audit age-related policies.

Explicit age-related policies

- In the health sector, there was a strong consensus that explicit age-related policies were on the decline.
- Most managers seemed to believe there were very few written policies specifying age criteria.
- There is likely to be a great deal more 'hidden discrimination', which has grown up through custom and practice.

Managers' understanding of age discrimination

- Some managers expressed confusion and uncertainty, both about the concept of age discrimination and about the criteria used to judge whether discrimination is either unfair or justified.
- This lack of clarity was most obvious when discussing the pros and cons of specialist services organised especially for older people, and clinicians' predisposition to under or over treat people of very advanced age.
- This confusion raises questions about senior managers' understanding of what to look for when 'rooting out age discrimination'.

Motivation to tackle age discrimination

- Action to combat age discrimination was frequently perceived by managers to be a low priority, compared with many other imperatives from Government.
- The number of complaints from older people about their care and treatment was also said to be low, and thus few managers felt any pressure for change from service users or the wider public.

Causes of age discrimination

The main underlying causes of age discrimination identified by respondents were:

- a lack of resources
- wider ageism inherent in society and the health and social services bureaucracy.

The difficulty in tackling these issues at a local level may explain some of the resignation expressed by some senior managers.

Action to combat age discrimination

- Managers revealed wide variations in the extent to which health and social care agencies have succeeded in involving older people in reviewing and developing local services.
- All managers of community health and social services knew of, and welcomed, the growth of older people's forums but they generally considered the involvement of older people in scrutinising policies and practices to be under-developed.
- Managers in acute hospitals were less committed and engaged with the public involvement agenda, and this was borne out by comparatively little evidence of activity.
- In line with Department of Health guidance, all managers were either actively engaged in or aware of steps being taken to put in place 'older people's champions' and local scrutiny groups required to implement the *NSF for Older People*.
- These arrangements were still at an early stage and far from completed in many places.

Conclusion

This survey suggests that efforts to 'root out age discrimination' in health and social care are taking place in a fertile climate of opinion.

- All the managers interviewed thought age discrimination was a 'bad thing' and they wanted to do something about it if it was shown to be a problem locally.
- The Government's stance on the unacceptability of age discrimination as laid out in the *NSF for Older People* appears to be an important driving force in stimulating and reinforcing action to combat unfair age discrimination in local services.

However, the approach of many senior managers is essentially reactive.

- Most are implementing, as required, the milestones set by the *NSF for Older People*.
- But few seem to be questioning the rationale for policies or practices that have evolved over many years, or taking the initiative to put an end to age discrimination in local services.
- This suggests that much more needs to be done to achieve radical changes in the way health and social care services are provided for older people.

Recommendations

The following strategies are recommended to combat further age discrimination. More work will be needed to develop these and the King's Fund will work with other interested bodies to develop these ideas further.

Clarification of the meaning and consequences of age discrimination

This will better equip managers and others in the health and social services sectors to identify age discrimination in their local services and to determine whether or not a particular policy or practice is justifiable.

The early development of benchmarking

This will help to detect hidden age discrimination, by enabling comparison of patterns of referral, treatment, care and support achieved in one locality with those in comparable areas.

Staff education and training

Better awareness of ageing and ageism should be included in educational programmes for staff at all levels. This is likely to need additional resources to ensure the development of appropriate course material and to provide sufficient opportunities for staff to reflect on their practice and change accordingly.

Critical assessment of specialist services provided for older people

Specialist services provided for older people should be critically assessed with the aim of eliminating policies that disadvantage older people by restricting access to good-quality care.

New age-equality legislation

New legislation is needed to outlaw age discrimination in health and social care, and to require local agencies to demonstrate that older people are not disadvantaged in terms of access to, or quality, of services provided.

Scrutiny of national social policies

This should challenge age-related policies and those policies that have a disproportionate effect on older people and may be indirectly discriminating against them.

Introduction

Age discrimination occurs at many levels from system-wide to the individual. There is much evidence to show there are two types of age discrimination – direct and indirect – in health and social care:[1]

- Direct discrimination – this occurs when an individual, or group of individuals, are treated differently because they are above or below a particular age.
- Indirect discrimination – this occurs when a service or practice has no explicit age bias, but still has a disproportionate impact on people in a particular age group.

Age discrimination is not necessarily unfair, with positive action being a well-established mechanism for addressing health inequalities. For example, free prescriptions are given to children and older people aged 60 and over, while specialist services for children, adolescents or older people can be a means of providing the most effective services for these client groups. Nevertheless, age discrimination is commonly understood to have a negative meaning and is therefore a sensitive subject area for service providers.

In older people, age discrimination, in its negative sense, may be caused by a lack of awareness of older people's needs rather than a deliberate intention to treat older people unfairly. It results from prejudice and stereotyped assumptions about older people, in which older people are viewed as a homogenous group characterised by:

- passivity
- failing physical and mental health
- dependency.

The Government and the National Service Framework for Older People

The publication of the *National Service Framework (NSF) for Older People*[2] by the Department of Health, in October 2000, underlined the Government's determination to tackle age discrimination in the health and social care services:

> *NHS services will be provided regardless of age, on the basis of clinical need alone. Social care services will not use age in their eligibility*

---

[1] Roberts E. *Age discrimination in health and social care.* (A briefing note). London: King's Fund, 2000 (unpublished).

[2] Department of Health. *National Service Framework for Older People.* London: HMSO, 2000.

criteria or policies to restrict access to available services.
(Standard One, *NSF for Older People*)

The *NSF for Older People* radically directs health and social care organisations to take a proactive approach to 'rooting out' discriminatory and ageist service provision. It also sets out tasks and targets that must be met to reach the NSF's standard on age discrimination (*see* Appendix A), including the appointment of clinical champions for older people, reviewing age-related policies and providing adequate training for staff to meet older people's needs.

Aims of the survey

The success of the Government's efforts to end age-discriminatory practices and of the *NSF for Older People* will depend very much on those responsible for putting the directive into action. This responsibility rests at the very highest levels of senior management in the NHS trusts and social services departments.

However, very little is known about how these managers perceive age discrimination and their response to it. The King's Fund therefore decided to conduct a telephone survey of senior managers in a range of health and social care organisations between June and August 2001.

Specifically, the survey aimed to discover:

- whether senior managers perceived age discrimination as affecting their local services and what form such discrimination took
- whether local organisations have the 'infrastructure' in place to deliver the NSF standard on age discrimination
- local examples of good practice in 'rooting out' age discrimination.

During the course of the telephone survey, participants were deliberately not given a definition of age discrimination before the interview and were free to bring their own perspective of the issue to the discussion.

Methods

Choice of sample frame

A sample of areas was identified using the Office of National Statistics (ONS) classification of local authority areas. This was stratified by a rural/urban split and weighted towards areas with a first- or second-wave primary care trust (PCT). The final sample of 25 areas is shown in Figure 1 below. The aim was to identify a diverse range of areas and organisations in England to be included in the survey.

Figure 1: Local authority areas included in the sample (shaded black)

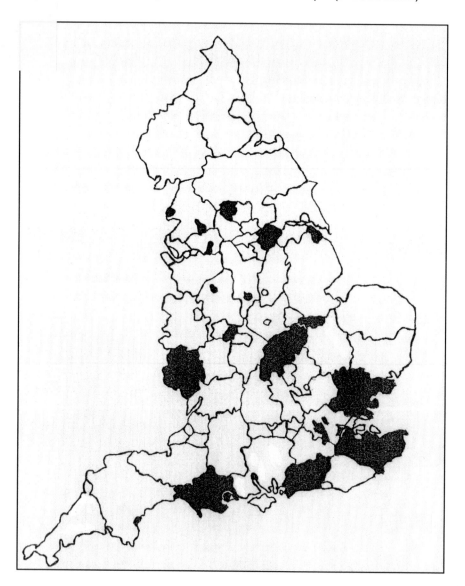

Within each area, one of each of the following types of providers was selected:

- primary care trust (PCT), or primary care group (PCG), if there was no first- or second-wave PCT
- community health or combined NHS trust
- acute NHS trust or combined NHS trust or single-specialty acute NHS trust
- social services department.

If there were insufficient NHS trusts in a sample area to meet the survey's quota, then substitute trusts were selected randomly from a list of NHS trusts in England.

Interviewees

In May 2001, a letter was sent to a total of 100 senior managers asking if they would take part in a telephone consultation about age discrimination (*see* Appendix B). The managers were assured that the consultation would be both voluntary and confidential. The letters were sent to:

- chief executives of PCT/Gs and community health NHS trusts
- medical directors of acute NHS trusts
- directors of social services in local authorities.

The letter was followed up with a telephone call about a week later. Those managers, initially contacted, who wanted to delegate the interview were allowed to choose their own nominee.

Interview

The interview was semi-structured, i.e. a series of general and open questions rather than a questionnaire. A pilot study, conducted with five senior managers in March and April 2001, had demonstrated that the questions were successful in prompting discussion and in drawing out different perceptions and experiences of age discrimination, as well as examples of good practice. The interviews were carried out in June by two interviewers who asked the same lead questions in the same order, with prompts. Details of the full interview are given in Appendix C. The written notes taken from the interviews were then analysed, drawing out emerging themes.

Results

We obtained a total of 75 interviews from the 100 managers approached initially, or their delegated interviewees; a response rate of 75 per cent. The managers interviewed represented a spread of experience in a diverse range of NHS trusts and social services departments across England. The response was very good in both the PCT/G sample (84 per cent) and community NHS trust sample (84 per cent) and in the social care sample (88 per cent). It was lower in the acute NHS trust sample (44 per cent). Overall, half of the interviews were delegated. Characteristics of the respondents are given in Appendix D.

Organisational context

Managers taking part in this survey were working in an environment characterised by organisational turbulence and financial pressures. The difficulties and uncertainties inherent in this environment emerged as managers talked about their roles and responsibilities regarding services for older people.

Primary care trusts (PCTs)

The PCTs in our sample were new organisations, with none being much more than 12 months old. One PCT had only been established in April 2001 and had not appointed all of its board members at the time of the interview in June.

The PCTs were characterised by small management and administrative staffing levels. They had a range of service responsibilities. Some of the PCTs were at 'Level 3', responsible for commissioning health services. Others had moved to 'Level 4', with a more extensive brief for providing services as well as commissioning them. Some PCTs also had the responsibility of managing premises, such as community hospitals and health centres, in addition to providing community-based nursing and therapies.

PCT chief executives who were interviewed had very wide-ranging roles. Delegated interviewees had various responsibilities, including managing staff, facilities and/or leading on strategic planning and development, while several of them were actually responsible for implementing the *NSF for Older People*, sometimes not just for their own PCT but on behalf of the health and local authorities as well.

Community NHS trusts

At the time of the interview, community services were undergoing devolution to the new PCTs. The community NHS trusts were therefore undergoing major organisational change, and either evolving into specialist mental health/learning disabilities trusts or preparing to be dissolved completely by April 2002. One of the trusts interviewed was a combined community, acute and mental health trust.

This organisational upheaval was reflected in the rapid revision of roles of some of our interviewees. For example, in one community trust being wound down, the interview was delegated to a manager, who it transpired during the interview, was already employed in a different organisation. Another interviewee described 'losing' staff to the new PCTs, but in turn, 'taking' staff from local mental health providers. This manager also said that his organisation was actively seeking to move to care trust status in the 'medium term'. This suggests that the organisational change for some community NHS trusts is unlikely to be resolved by 2002.

Acute and specialist NHS trusts

Acute and specialist NHS trusts tended to be much more stable in terms of the scope and range of services provided. Nevertheless, one trust had recently undergone a major reorganisation of acute services and merged with another trust earlier in the year.

The response to the interview was poorer among acute NHS trusts compared with the community and social care sectors, with only 11 out of 25 (44 per cent) acute NHS trusts agreeing to participate. However, the responding acute NHS trusts comprised a diverse range of organisations, covering rural and urban locations, university teaching hospitals, a hospital split over separate sites, a large combined NHS trust and one single specialty hospital. One hospital served a large retired population on the south coast of England, with the medical director feeling that the trust had developed a considerable expertise in caring for older inpatients.

With one exception, the eight medical directors interviewed had continued working part-time as consultants. The three medical directors who delegated their interview did so to consultant colleagues. Thus, these interviews provide some insight into medical perceptions of age discrimination.

Social services departments

The social services departments included in the survey were demographically and geographically diverse. In organisational terms, they were established 'players' with a long experience of commissioning and providing services for older people.

There was much less mention of the potential benefits of greater structural integration of health and social services than among interviewees in the primary and community trust samples. However, one interviewee was both a joint director of social services and chief executive of the health authority.

Several local authorities had changed the way they were structured from a committee to a cabinet style of working. Some social services departments had been reorganised to separate strategic and provider roles. One of the interviewees was accountable directly to elected council members rather than the director of social services; this may have enabled the respondent to act seemingly quickly to implement change.

The impact of budget constraints on service quality was a consistent and obvious theme. The financial constraints on social services were also often referred to in the PCT and community trust interviews, usually while discussing working in partnership with social services.

Presence of age discrimination in local services

The first part of the interview asked for managers' subjective assessment of whether age discrimination occurred within their services. Interviewees were not provided before the interview with a definition of age discrimination.

Most managers (75 per cent) believed that age discrimination was taking place in some form or other within services in their local area. Only about 25 per cent thought age discrimination was unlikely in their local services, though this was often qualified with comments about the difficulty in spotting it:

> *We don't discriminate on age. I'm not 100 per cent sure it never happens.* (Assistant director of social services)

> *For the sort of work we do, many of the . . . diseases affect the elderly, I wouldn't have thought we discriminate.* (Hospital consultant)

> *We don't commission services like that, there are no specific bars.* (Assistant director, PCT)

Some managers seemed uncomfortable with the term 'age discrimination', and several of the interviewees were guarded in tone. One respondent in social services felt that the age discrimination debate was associated with left-wing politics and this was an important consideration when working with elected members.

Examples of age-related policies or age bars

Most of the examples of age discrimination described by senior managers in their local services were direct discrimination, in which policies restricted access to particular units, facilities and treatments by setting upper or lower age limits (Appendix E). However, it was consistently said that there were very few written policies specifying age criteria or age bar:

> *Going back ten years, we used to have cut-off points, now 94- and 95-year-olds come in.* (Medical director, acute hospital trust)

No written policies use age as a determining factor. The only way to find out would be to undertake a piece of comparative work looking at referrals, prescribing, etc. (Director of primary care, PCT)

Managers in the community trust sample were most likely to identify explicit age-related services. Interviewees often considered such restrictions to be rational, though the respondents did not always personally agree with the underlying reason. For example, one specialist neuro-rehabilitation service limited its programme to people under 65 because of its emphasis on returning people to work.

Among both the community and primary care respondents, chiropody was said to be the most common service said to discriminate by age. It tended to have minimum rather than maximum age limits for access. Older people were not necessarily identified as the main group at risk in this case and neither was discrimination necessarily felt to be unfair.

Indeed, in the community trust sample, older people were more often identified as having better access to appropriate services because community services tended to be designed for patients in older age groups. A common observation was that older people were the 'core business' or the main user group of community services.

Very few examples of indirect discrimination were given, and these reflected some of the major concerns expressed in general by older people, such as limited availability of particular kinds of surgery, drugs and equipment. Interviewees' understanding of the concept of indirect discrimination was often hazy, though not always. The interviews were peppered with qualifications such as ' . . . if you could call that discrimination'.

Audits of age-related policies

Virtually all the respondents knew that the *NSF for Older People* specified local audits of age-related policies. In June when these interviews were undertaken, such audits, which were carried out in all of the respondents' trusts, had not been completed. It is therefore unknown how the examples of age-related access to services listed in Appendix E will have been affected by audits carried out since the interview.

Reasons given for restricting services by age

Respondents were more likely to describe age criteria as having 'evolved' rather than as a deliberate strategy to ration services. An exception was a community trust, which had, until recently, limited some stroke and rehabilitation services because of 'volume of demand' to people under 65, even though most patients needing the service were over 65. The health authority had recently funded this service up to age 75.

One PCT chief executive believed rationing by age was justified in principle (though he was not aware that it occurred within his PCT's services), because he believed that younger people had a greater claim to finite resources for life-threatening conditions. He was the only respondent of 75 to articulate this view.

Generally, however, managers gave a very different reason for restricting community health services by age. Minimum age criteria acted as a form of protection for older people to ensure access to services in high demand:

> *It's a method of rationing, for example, [the] continence [budget] is always overspent . . . You create age criteria to reflect the level of demand, and because users in the older age brackets may not have the same 'voice' as younger users.* (Chief executive, community trust)

Few interviewees used the term 'rationing'. Nevertheless, one of the most common explanations given for age discrimination (direct or indirect) was competing priorities for insufficient resources.

Specialist services for older people and other age groups

Services are often organised and funded for particular age groups, e.g. as in special wards, units, centres or care homes, clinical specialties, or approaches to care. Concerns about specialisation were expressed throughout the interviews, particularly for social services, paediatric, and adolescent and mental health services. Both younger, middle-aged people (e.g. those with early-onset dementia) and older people were identified as being potentially disadvantaged by restricted access to services. One interviewee noted that older people themselves had challenged the 'rigid requirement' to move from adult mental health services to older people's services at age 65.

Social services provision

Social services are typically organised and funded around different age groups (i.e. children, young adults and older people), with older people being by far the largest single 'client group'. This division of services is intended to differentiate (i.e. discriminate) between different groups with different needs, and social services interviewees were therefore asked about the level of provision given to different client groups.

Allocation of resources by age

Although some interviewees felt these divisions can lead to unfair treatment of older people because of, for example, lower levels of funding for services used by older people, not all respondents believed that older people were being treated unfairly. Several respondents said that the different cost ceilings for community care packages reflected the different 'markets' for residential care. Thus, since fewer residential places were needed for younger disabled adults, they tended to be more expensive, with local authorities having little influence over the level of fees for these services:

> *We don't discriminate . . . There are different cost ceilings but that's based on market values. Doesn't stop anyone getting access to services.* (Director, social services)

Another respondent saw the presence of differential cost ceilings as reflecting positive discrimination in favour of younger people rather than negative provision for older people:

> *Historically, we have [over]spent . . . on learning disabilities. We had a lot of large institutions and had to move people . . . as part of community care reforms. So it's more that we've had to positively discriminate in favour of people with learning disabilities.* (Director, social services)

Other respondents were less reassuring. They suggested that older people were more likely than other clients to be placed in residential care or to have less choice over care options. Reference to the market is again made by one of the following interviewees, but all three respondents also acknowledge that the approach of social services to older people is inherently discriminatory. The examples given point to differences in service provision from resource allocation and commissioning through to assessment of need at the individual level:

> *The limit for younger disabled is much higher . . . because residential costs are higher. The market for older people is more 'pile em high, sell 'em cheap'. But also . . . there's a notion of 'it's more important to keep a young person at home'.* (Head of older people's strategy)

> *It's [age discrimination] very noticeable when assessing the needs of younger persons . . . 'Do they have a social life?' and so on. For older people, we take a much more basic view.* (Director, social services)

> *Generally . . . there's less per head for older people. It's historical, when local authorities were charged with eligibility criteria there was great concern about the consequences of an open-ended approach. [Older people are] placed in residential care homes so we don't overspend. It's discrimination because it's not how we would treat . . . children, then it's 'hang the cost'.* (Director, social services)

Historical ageism

Some interviewees expressed the view that historical patterns of service provision have a tendency to become 'norms' for current and future care. Thus, historical attitudes may become part of the culture of service provision and therefore 'invisible' to some extent and difficult to tackle:

> *The obvious comparison is with mental health 50 years ago and the large Victorian asylums. Older people's services are still suffering from the asylum mentality.* (Intermediate care co-ordinator)

> *We expect to pay significantly higher amounts for residential care for younger adults. It's historical, based on lower expectations . . . Some of that will be realistic and some is 'that's the way we've always done it'.* (Director, social services)

> *Our response is age-related. We think it isn't but if you stand back . . .* (Manager, social services adult provision)

Acute and community health services

Specialist services for older people are also a feature of acute and community health services. The debate about whether general or specialist models of care are more appropriate for older people was particularly apparent in the interviews with medical directors. There were conflicting views:

> *It's very well integrated now, general medicine and geriatric medicine . . . We can make certain about not missing diagnoses.* (Medical director, acute NHS trust)

> *In the past, anyone over 70 was admitted to the medical elderly ward. Now all emergency admissions go to [the] acute assessment unit for immediate treatment and then the appropriate ward. It works better. We want medicine of the elderly to disappear [and] to develop . . . a specialism in multi-organ disease or rehabilitation.* (Medical director, acute NHS trust)

> *[There is] medical justification for age-based criteria. The elderly have multi-pathologies. Physicians [caring for the elderly] have a broader perspective than generalists.* (Medical director, combined trust)

Other respondents singled out dedicated elderly wards as the focus for excellent care of the elderly in their organisations, in contrast to the level of skill and knowledge on more general wards. For example, 'most junior doctors at ward level haven't a clue [how to care well for older patients]' (Medical director, acute NHS trust). Furthermore, according to one manager from the PCT sample, older people admitted to general wards in their area, following the closure of local dedicated elderly wards, were at greater risk of neglect.

Arbitrary nature of age cut-off points

Many of the interviewees questioned not so much the specialisation of services as the arbitrary nature of using age to define boundaries:

> *People can have co-morbidities at any age, and if you don't qualify, then you miss out.* (Specialist services manager, community trust)

> *A 65 or so cut-off is arbitrary . . . The biggest client group is 80 plus – very few people under this age are getting older people's services. . . The over-75 or over-80 age group [needs] a special focus rather than a simple age cut-off.* (Director, social services)

Some respondents believed that the way in which services were commissioned and delivered caused these arbitrary age cut-offs. Services were being designed with age groups in mind rather than around individuals' needs: 'the pathways are nonsensical'. (Specialist services manager, community trust)

> *There are services only for the elderly as well as some only for the young. [Discrimination] is fairly systematic and institutionalised . . . embedded by commissioning and the way this is approached. Users are viewed as client groups – we don't think of a person's journey through life.* (Chief executive, PCT)

> *It's a cultural thing, left over from the purchaser-provider days, [which] encouraged a focus on younger patients, because it was better value for money. Things are changing, consultants' attitudes are changing – they are more willing to treat elders.* (Chief executive, PCT)

A nursing manager in a community trust said there were no explicit age-related exclusion criteria in services, just 'non-thinking discrimination . . . people are working in silos – they didn't plan services as a whole'. Thus, services for younger physically disabled patients operated up until 60, while the geriatric services normally included people over 75.

But would removing cut-offs be enough to ensure a truly needs-related service? Another respondent felt that ageist attitudes on the part of health service staff meant that access to services was sometimes needs-related in name only:

> *[Professionals] don't do enough of assessing need, they see the age first.* (Joint commissioning manager, health authority/social services)

Staff's flexible interpretation of age cut-off points

Many respondents stressed that age limits to specialist services were interpreted flexibly by staff. Many services accepted referrals that breached age criteria according to the individual patient:

> *[There is no] real evidence that . . . policies militate against doing something. A person's capabilities, competencies and support [are all considered].* (Chief executive, community trust)

Nevertheless, the very existence of age criteria seems designed to limit professional autonomy over access:

> *We do have benchmarking [of care package costs by client group]. It's pretty rare that we go outside that. When you're 85 plus, there's a tendency to be offered the mainstream.*
> (Assistant director, adult social services)

High-level need versus preventive services

Social care is increasingly targeted on people with the greatest need. Several interviewees pointed out negative consequences for older people. The first respondent quoted below believes that the lack of low-level preventive services discriminates against the 'younger old', who have less access to statutory support because resources are being targeted towards those with highest need. According to both respondents, the lack of preventive support leads to irreversible loss of independence so further disadvantaging individuals as they get older:

> *Resources targeted towards the most in need and not towards lesser priorities discriminates against younger older people [so that] more people are at greater risk of breakdown. There is no satisfactory formula [to quantify the effectiveness of more preventive approaches].*
> (Director, social services)

> *We've got a declining number of people on statutory provision and a growing population of older people – and what are we providing? Two hours of home care a week [for older people] . . . Even preventive services are about avoiding high-dependency cases – they aren't truly preventive at all.* (Director, social services)

These respondents also gave examples of local initiatives with a preventive impact that they felt had some potential to tackle these issues. These examples were aimed at helping older people to maintain and develop social networks and to keep fit and active by, for example, opening school swimming pools to older people, or providing back up for older people's luncheon clubs.

Clinical decision-making: 'do not resuscitate' policy

Many interviewees referred to age discrimination within clinical decision-making. This was often mentioned in the context of 'do not resuscitate' (DNR) policy and practice. Respondents did not usually have daily experience of such a policy, but they were strongly aware of the way in which DNR had been linked with age discrimination by the media and Age Concern.[3,4]

Although medical managers tended to disagree that the concept of DNR policy was discriminatory in principle, there was some discussion about the uncertainties involved in assessing risk and outcome in individual older patients:

> *When I trained as a surgeon, you didn't operate on anyone over 60; it was the perceived wisdom and the results were appalling. The problem now is that there's no evidence base even though we have an ageing population . . . 60 is not old any more. You have to go on gut feeling [in deciding whether to operate].* (Medical director, acute trust)

> *It's not so much age discrimination as the diseases that present at a certain age . . . So take someone at 90, there's not much [we can do] . . . at the age of 45, we can do something . . . [The age at which doctors start to question the options] it's changing over time but it does still apply.* (Medical director, acute trust)

It is almost certainly true that older people's levels of health and fitness have improved with rising standards of living. The fact that '60 isn't old any more' implies a subjective element to clinical (and wider social) evaluations of quality of life in older age, and touches on a central issue behind the public furore over DNR – to what extent are doctors making clinical judgements based on prejudiced assessments of age-related risk? However, this interview was not an appropriate tool to explore this topic properly.

The evidence we collected was frequently reflective. One medical director described the difficulties inherent, even in shared clinical decision-making:

> *At a meeting, I often say – should we be offering chemo [therapy] to this person of 85 – should we give them that option? . . . But isn't it our job to take on that decision? Patients say 'What would you do if it was you, doctor?' They don't know. Sometimes you see people suffer, and it does them no good . . . it's a very difficult balance.*
> (Medical director, acute trust)

---

[3] Boseley S: Call to outlaw medical ageism. *The Guardian*, 28 April 2000.

[4] Department of Health. *Government reinforces patients' rights on resuscitation decisions.* Press Release 2000/0490, 5 September 2000.

Equality of access to acute care

Concerning access to hospital care, acute NHS trust respondents felt there was relatively little scope (or incentive) for them to discriminate against older people as the trusts had little control over referrals. Not one of the interviewees thought older people were denied access to hospital care, in any deliberate way, because of their age. Occasionally, however, respondents suspected that primary care referrals might be biased towards younger patients:

> *Four or five years ago, GPs still didn't have to refer [for cataract] unless patients were practically blind. Now, that's considered poor practice and it's beginning to change, particularly for children.*
> (Medical director, acute NHS trust)

Interestingly, the concept of the acute hospital as a 'fixer' was quite striking in the interviews with medical managers – 'we do them all – young or old'– who often employed industrial or mechanical metaphors in their accounts of hospital work.

Role of GPs as gatekeepers to hospital care

Interestingly, in our interviews with PCT managers, the role of GPs as gatekeepers was not often raised. Even though we did not ask specifically about this aspect of care, it is perhaps surprising it was not mentioned more often, particularly as a national survey of GPs had recently been published suggesting disturbing levels of age discrimination among GPs.[5] This may be because practice-level data, e.g. referral patterns by age, tends not to be systematically monitored by PCT managers or, indeed, by anyone.

One respondent from an acute NHS trust felt strongly that discrimination was more tangible in the way older people were viewed after admission. 'People are very well managed in the first few days.' But after their initial treatment, she felt that doctors were quick to discharge older patients to residential care, without much thought of the long-term outcomes for the patient or their wishes.

> *[That is the key] decision where patients are not involved and it annoys me more than [older people's] treatment in hospital.*
> (Medical director, acute NHS trust)

---

[5] Age Concern England. *Two-thirds of GPs back call for inquiry into ageist NHS.* Press Release. 17 May 2000.

Attitudes to caring for older people in hospital

Another medical director from an acute NHS trust wondered if the reality of caring for people with chronic or multiple health problems fell short of the acute professionals' expectations of curing people:

> *Geriatric wards are not popular with staff . . . There are a lot of people for whom you can't do that much. It's not why they [staff] come into hospital work.* (Medical director, acute NHS trust)

This view was not limited solely to the hospital sector, as demonstrated by a primary care manager from a PCT:

> *If the prognosis is poor for an older person or if they might not achieve the desired outcomes, this can affect staff attitudes.*
> (Primary care manager, PCT)

Although there was little obvious evidence or examples of restricted access to acute hospital care, there were some concerns about how well acute hospitals were serving older people's needs – a more subtle form of discrimination:

> *A lot of government policies prioritise intermediate care . . . [it seems that older people] don't deserve acute medicine.*
> (Consultant geriatrician, acute NHS trust)

Quality of care at the end of life

Quality of care at the end of life was one of the services singled out for criticism. Two of the medical directors cited examples of heroic interventions which they ascribed to colleague's fears of being labelled ageist, but which prevented people from dying with dignity. Sometimes, the capacity of specialist palliative care services was questioned.

Managers' confidence in health and social care services

Near the end of the interview, managers were asked how confident they would feel about their local health and social care services if they themselves were an older person. This question prompted managers to think about services as a whole, taking the user's perspective. The response was mixed and best summed up by the respondent who was confident that local services:

> *would meet my needs, but perhaps, not in the way I would want them to be met.* (Director, social services)

Managers tended to be more confident about the services provided by their own organisation or services in their own locality than in other agencies or areas, reflecting their knowledge of their own systems and structures.

Respondents from the acute NHS trust sample were especially confident about clinical standards of care. However, this was qualified by concerns about 'process issues', e.g. discharge, and also about the lack of 'creature comforts' in hospital:

> *I would bet that if they [the elderly] come into the care of the elderly wards, they won't like it. But I think we're providing the best care we can.* (Medical director, acute NHS hospital)

Several themes emerged consistently in people's answers to this question, echoing earlier concerns.

Access to care

Access was again an issue for some respondents. People cited complex pathways, poor communication about services and, much more rarely, limited capacity:

> *The access to orthopaedic services is poor and funding is restricted. The amount of care is less than it was and entry-gate criteria are higher. The pot of social services money is not purchasing enough care but once you're into the service, elders will have a different view, it will seem better.* (Chief executive, community trust)

Knowledge of the system

Knowledge of the system was often thought to be important to obtain access to good care and obviously respondents felt that they were relatively well placed in this regard. Respondents with direct experience of family members in receipt of long-term care or in sheltered housing tended to be the most confident.

Role of family and carers

The role of family members and informal carers in providing long-term care was acknowledged. There was some fear of becoming a 'burden' to one's family and, more rarely expressed, about the ageing process itself.

'Slipping through the net'

Criticisms about gaps in services, poor integration and patchy provision (especially for black and minority ethnic elders) were made. A comment made several times was the risk of 'slipping through the net':

> *For nursing care there are three different teams. During the week two different carers go into people's homes four times per day – who's going*

to review that? There is no care co-ordination between health and social care for older people. (Head of elderly services, community trust)

Other themes

One of the most striking feature of people's answers was the consistency with which respondents believed that their own needs were more likely to be met because the ageing post-war generation will demand greater respect from society and will be less tolerant of poor services.

In addition, several respondents in social services and community samples stressed the lack of early and preventive services, and of support that addressed isolation and loneliness. Respondents also identified lifetime opportunities as an important factor, particularly in terms of social care. For example, older people with an occupational pension were in a better position to fund good-quality care. There was some perception of statutory social care services as a safety net for poorer older people.

Perceptions of older people and their families

We asked interviewees if patients and older people had voiced concerns about age discrimination within services. Although health service managers cited individual complaints about discriminatory behaviour (often by patients' relatives on their behalf), there seemed to be very little local agitation about age discrimination from older people themselves.

Patients' relatives were identified both as older patients' champions but also as a source of conflict. Relatives were perceived sometimes to have unrealistic expectations or to attempt to influence treatment decisions to their own advantage. One respondent identified the 'flak' that nurses receive from patients' relatives to be sufficient to deter nursing staff from working on dedicated elderly hospital wards.

Older people's expectations of services

A very consistent theme across the whole sample was that older people's expectations of services were low:

> *People are not very good at going out and asking . . . and the services aren't that good at finding unmet need . . . there isn't enough chiropody or rehabilitation. If you want any physical refurbishment done to your home, like stair rails, you can wait a very long time.*
> (Head of primary care, PCT)

A service development manager of a PCT gave an example drawn from her previous work as a district nurse. When she rang older people to make an appointment to visit, none of her patients would state a preferred time; they just expressed relief she was visiting at all.

Finally, one interviewee made the following comment, though stated humorously, about accessing statutory services should she ever need them:

> *I'm going to be awful, really demanding.* (Manager, community trust)

This reflects the double standard faced by older people. Low expectations of care may be self-fulfilling, but conversely if people do demand services to which they are entitled, they may find themselves labelled as 'difficult'.

Initiatives for tackling age discrimination

Infrastructure

Wide variations were reported in the extent to which health and social care organisations have established an infrastructure capable of systematically scrutinising services and taking action to deal with unfair age discrimination.

Older people's forums

Some organisations were much more experienced than others in involving older people and their organisations in reviewing policies and practices. All the managers of community health and social services were aware of local groups and forums that regularly worked with their local councils or NHS trusts in strategic planning and service development. However, even where older people's forums had been established for some time, many managers tended to believe that mechanisms for hearing the views and experiences of older people were markedly underdeveloped. A common refrain was, 'We could always do more.' Managers in acute trusts were far less engaged with public involvement processes.

Response to the *National Service Framework for Older People*

All the interviewees said that the milestones of the *NSF for Older People* were being implemented locally. However, the pace of implementation varied. Typically, interviewees said that age discrimination had been discussed at board level with implementation being facilitated through working groups – often with other health and social care agencies. Many organisations had already appointed older people's champions, and steps were being taken to implement the audit of age-related policies. It was this latter task that seemed to cause the most comment. The timetable was frequently criticised ('absurd'), as was the lack of timely guidance that had been promised by the Department of Health.

Policy initiatives: local examples

We asked respondents to describe any other initiatives taking place that, in their opinion, tackled age discrimination. Most of the examples were of attempts to improve the availability and quality of services for older people (*see* Table 1), but there were also examples directly aimed at tackling discrimination (*see* Table 2).

However, examples of good practice or improved services for older people that were thought likely to tackle age discrimination indirectly were much more common. Interviewees in the community health and social services sample often identified a shift in the culture of provision, which one respondent described as 'enabling rather than nurturing', and a greater focus on maintaining older people's independence. There was considerable optimism and enthusiasm about the quality of care provided under these initiatives.

National policy developments

National policy developments have also clearly had been influential. In addition to the NSF, respondents cited the following as significant levers for change for older people in their localities:

- 'Best Value' reviews in local government – particularly when the review cut across departmental boundaries
- Better Government for Older People
- Some respondents, particularly within PCTs and community trusts, were positive about the potential of greater structural integration through the Health Act Flexibilities and Care Trusts
- Health Action Zones
- Beacon status
- In the NHS, *Improving Working Lives Standard* [6] strategy on good employment practice.

---

[6] Department of Health. *Improving Working Lives Standard*. London: HMSO, 2000.

Table 1: Examples of ways in which age discrimination is being tackled locally

Service development	Objective/benefit
Social services sample	
• Direct payments to older people	Promotes user choice and autonomy
• Action based research projects by staff	Staff development and awareness
• 'Softening' eligibility criteria	Fairer access to services
• Best Value reviews on social inclusion and community safety (different councils)	Systematic and cross cutting approach to issues
• 'Grandparents initiative' (Sure Start scheme)	Benefits for young people
• Specialist home care team for dementia	High-quality care
• Beacon award for mental health services	High-quality care
PCT sample	
• Community transport between health sites	Making services accessible
• Intermediate care investment (noted by several respondents)	Promoting independence
• Joint action on cataract services	Expanding access to surgery
• Adult protection strategy	Prevent and tackle elder abuse
• Co-ordinating care of terminally ill at primary/secondary interface	Promotes choice and control
• Specialist service for Irish elders	Addresses specific needs of this group
Community trust sample	
• Intermediate care (noted by several respondents)	Promoting independence
• Re-ablement and rapid response teams	Promoting independence
• Innovation in nursing homes	High-quality care
• Organisational development: 'leading empowered organisations'	Positive organisational culture
• Audit of physical disability services	Identifying gaps in services
• New unit with 50 rehabilitation beds	Investment in high-quality care

Table 2: Summary of initiatives established against age discrimination

Staff education and training
• Training for staff, which includes components on the needs of older people such as the National Vocational Qualification (NVQ) for assistants
• Some diversity and cultural awareness training, again including a focus on age, as well as race, ethnic diversity and disability
Social inclusion and citizenship
• Examples cited by the managers in social services which directly attempted to tackle discrimination tended to be council-wide initiatives, e.g. looking at ways in which older people could participate in community networks, libraries, and leisure facilities
• Schemes bringing older people together with children and adolescents. In one example, this was with the intention of addressing ageist stereotypes of both young and old
• Respondents who reported investment in community and intergenerational relationships were very positive about the potential impact for older people's independence
Employment policies
• Equal opportunities policies frequently mentioned age. However, it was not always clear to what extent policy was being implemented or monitored in this respect
• Primary care trusts and community trusts seemed to be the most flexible employers, many operating 'bank' systems for staff interested in working part-time after retirement

Discussion

Age discrimination identified in local services

The survey results suggest that older people are at risk of unfair discrimination both in health and social care services. Only about 25 per cent of respondents denied that access to or quality of services was related to age. The remainder provided examples of both direct and indirect age discrimination. These did not discriminate solely against the elderly, but adversely affected patients and clients of all ages, particularly with regard to age-related restrictions. However, age discrimination was also perceived as a method of positive discrimination: age-based criteria were seen to favour older people or were viewed as a reasonable proxy of need or specialism. In addition, older people's access to the same types of services varied in different parts of the country.

Respondents in the social services sample were the most consistent in identifying 'institutional' discrimination, i.e. discrimination inherent in service design. Several social services respondents commented that despite their goals to the contrary, older people's services promoted dependency and offered people very limited choices.

Tackling age discrimination

One of the main contradictions in our findings has been that while the interviews did point to various forms of age discrimination, this was rarely seen as a local priority for management action. The *NSF for Older People* was being implemented, but this was being driven by national directives rather than any local imperatives. However, it would be wrong to portray respondents as insensitive or unreflective about services: there was a great deal of enthusiasm in the way that most respondents talked about older people and services.

The most common factors underlying age discrimination identified in the interviews were:

- lack of resources
- widespread ageism in society
- the legacy of historical ageism in the welfare state.

Clearly, the difficulty in addressing these issues at a local level may explain some of the resignation that prevailed in our sample about tackling age discrimination. But there were additional reasons why age discrimination was difficult to address:

- There seemed to be considerable confusion about when age discrimination was justified and when it was not. This was most obvious in the conversations with PCT, community trust and acute trust managers about specialist versus generalist services where specialist services were defined by an age range rather than a medical or social condition.

- In addition, some managers' understanding of indirect discrimination was unclear, and statements were often qualified with comments such as ' . . . if you could call that discrimination'.

- Examples of 'heroic' interventions were ascribed to medical colleagues' fears of being labelled ageist. These examples (although anecdotal rather than based on personal experience) demonstrate that being treated equally can be interpreted as meaning everyone should get the same resources, intervention or service.

- Age discrimination is a relative concept, and involves identifying 'winners' as well as 'losers'. This concept was not only difficult to understand sometimes but, to some extent, was also uncomfortable for managers responsible for providing services to communities as a whole, where services may have conflicting priorities.

- In social services, it was considered that the relative volume of older people as a client group was a barrier to action, and that redistributing resources more equitably would result in little benefit to individuals. The concern about this argument is that it could, in theory, be used to justify reductions or incursions into social services' budgets for older people. However, there is no evidence from this survey to support this notion.

- Some interviewees were uncomfortable with the term 'age discrimination', especially as it is usually seen as being negative, and, not surprisingly, several respondents were guarded in tone. Age discrimination is also a politicised issue, with one respondent in social services associating the discrimination debate with left-wing politics – an important consideration when working, as in this case, with elected members on a Conservative council.

- The difficulty many managers reported in identifying ageism at the level of the individual professional–patient encounter seemed to encourage a view of age discrimination as an abstract phenomenon.

Certainly, in the community health and social services samples, concepts such as citizenship, inclusion and independence were sometimes regarded as more productive ways of approaching many of the same issues about accessibility, quality and outcomes experienced by older people and patients.

Nevertheless, we would argue that age discrimination with its explicit connotation of 'unfairness' is important. Its power comes from the way that it directly challenges our assumptions about older people. In this survey, a relatively brief interview over the telephone yielded many insights into the ways in which services may unfairly affect older people.

The importance of the National Service Framework for Older People

In all of the interviews, it was clear that steps were being taken to implement the NSF in respect to age discrimination. Furthermore, almost without exception, respondents thought that the NSF's explicit reference to age discrimination was a good thing for older people. However, interviewees were resentful about the time-scale of implementation, the delay in getting guidance on reviewing age-related policies, the number of competing central initiatives and the lack of additional resources. Several respondents accused the Government of double standards in not itself reviewing age-related criteria in national policy, e.g. in social security regulations.

However, it is important to note that this policy does not simply articulate a principle as has happened with previous statements from the Government and professional bodies. It goes much further in requiring organisations to take action to root out discrimination. This, in turn, means that health and social care organisations will be more directly accountable to older people on the grounds of equity in their provision of services to this patient group.

Conclusion

During the course of this survey, we were given many examples of recent or current service developments, commitment to public involvement and partnership working that were likely to have particular benefit, either directly or indirectly, for older people and carers. Many respondents spoke with enthusiasm and, in some cases, with passion. Improving services so that they better meet the needs and aspirations of older people (and carers) will in itself have an impact on age discrimination.

However, the gap between managers' awareness of various forms of age discrimination in services and its comparative low priority for action suggest that age discrimination is not yet widely seen as 'an issue for all of us'. The *NSF for Older People*, with its emphasis on written policies (which from the evidence of this survey are already on the decline), will not challenge ageist organisational cultures, structures and attitudes, in the short term at least, and further strategies are required.

Recommendations

We believe the following recommendations are likely to have a positive impact on age discrimination given the evidence from the survey. However, these may not necessarily be straightforward to implement well nor are they quick fixes. There are also likely to be drawbacks or adverse consequences, which need to be evaluated to a greater degree than is possible here, given the qualitative nature of our survey.

Clarify the meaning and consequences of age discrimination

In view of the confusion around this form of inequality, managers and, we suspect, others charged with combating age discrimination in health and social care would be helped by guidance setting out a conceptual framework for spotting and challenging policies and practices that disadvantage older people. Work underway at the Institute for Public Policy may be helpful, especially if its work could be made accessible and usable by both lay and professional audiences alike.

Develop benchmarking

The *NSF for Older People* promises the development of a benchmarking process to allow referral and service patterns to be compared between different organisations. The evidence from our survey suggests that development of benchmarking should be high priority, as many respondents found it very difficult to identify age discrimination at the individual level. Analysing aggregate patterns of treatment for possible age bias is one way of detecting unwritten discrimination. Such data monitoring was extremely rare among our respondents, with only two mentioning any sort of data-mapping exercise. A start could be made on those aspects of health and social care that are particularly important for older people, e.g. hip replacements, cataract removals or aids for independent living.

Introduce age-equality legislation

By explicitly acknowledging discrimination, the *NSF for Older People* legitimises older people's right to raise discrimination as a strategic issue. But does the NSF go far enough? The survey provides little direct evidence on this. Only one respondent volunteered legal action as an effective way of tackling discrimination. However, legislation that outlawed age discrimination in services and put the onus on organisations to demonstrate they did not discriminate would exert more pressure on managers to change discriminatory practices than can the *NSF for Older People*.

Current UK legislation concerning age discrimination in statutory services is very weak. Under the European Convention on Human Rights (ratified under UK law in 2000), people can legally challenge discrimination only if the consequences have adversely affected their right to life, family, privacy, etc, and stronger legislation banning age discrimination is urgently required. However, the time may be right to introduce stronger legislation, together with implementation of the EU Framework Directive prohibiting discrimination in employment and occupation on grounds of age. This must be implemented by EU member states, including the UK, by 2006, and could provide the Government with an opportunity to extend anti-age discrimination legislation to health and social care. At the same time, there would be some merit in overhauling current equalities legislation concerning race, sex and disability, on the lines suggested by Lord Lester at the recent Help the Aged annual lecture.[7]

Care will need to be taken in any legislation affecting access to health care to avoid introducing perverse incentives for staff and professionals to act 'defensively' to minimise their risk of being sued rather than maximise their patients' best interests and wishes.

Scrutinise national policy

Besides a lack of resources, managers most commonly identified an inherently ageist society and bureaucracy as a main barrier to tackling age discrimination. Both factors are not easily amenable to local intervention. If the Government is serious about tackling age discrimination, it should make more effort to review national age-related policies, perhaps along the lines suggested in the *NSF for Older People*. This would encourage serious consideration of age-based policies across a wide spectrum of social policies. Such scrutiny would also challenge any policies that indirectly disadvantage older people, such as those relating to long-term care, and that reinforce discriminatory policies and practices at a local level.

Invest in staff education and training

Some managers identified training as a strategy for tackling age discrimination. Typically, the courses described tended to be aimed at front-line staff and postgraduate clinical professionals. However, professional colleges and bodies may need to consider reviewing the pre-qualification training and education given to health and social care professionals.

Older people comprise the largest consumers of health and social care. Diversity training in these sectors should include a component on age and should also be provided to staff at all levels of health and social care organisations, not just those in direct care roles.

---

[7] Lester A. Age discrimination and equality. Help the Aged Annual Lecture, 2001.

Although much can be done to build awareness of ageing and ageism into existing educational programmes at minimal cost to the organisations concerned, additional resources will be needed to stimulate the development of appropriate course material and to enable staff to have the time to reflect on their practice away from work.

Critically assess specialist services provided to older people

Specialisation of services clearly brings many benefits, especially in developing skills and expertise. However, the rationale for attaching specific age cut-offs, even to specialist services, is difficult to understand, particularly when respondents talked about the need for flexibility at the margins.

For example, why are mental health services for older people deemed to start at age 65 when the overwhelming majority of users will be much older and would be much better characterised by their particular mental and social care needs? Elderly mental health was a specialty that was criticised perhaps more than any other by interviewees. The rationale behind providing a separate category of mental health services for older people is that they will receive better care as a result but this did not seem convincingly so in this survey.

There was clear controversy about the benefits and disadvantages of generic compared with specialist old age services in the acute sector. It was not clear in our interviews if specialist older people's services were being included in the NSF reviews of age-related policies. If age cut-offs are felt to be a useful guide for particular services, then there ought to be an explicit policy statement (subject to review under the terms of the NSF) that justifies this position for older clients, patients and their families. Furthermore, age cut-offs should reflect the age range of the targeted client group. Non-critical use of a notional retirement age as a basis for defining specialist services should be unacceptable.

Appendix A

National Service Framework for Older People: key objectives

Raising the priority of older people's services
• Older people's champions should be established in all health and social care organisations
• Organisations are expected to select a non-executive director or elected council member to take on this role
• Clinical champions will be appointed for older people
Representation and involvement of older people
• All agencies should seek to engage older people
• Patients' Forums in the NHS should be representative of users and will have a designated older people's champion
Review of age-related policies
• By 1 October 2001, all health and social care agencies should have scrutinised relevant policies for age bias, including council eligibility criteria for social care
• The results will be published in the annual report
• From April 2002, any action arising from these reviews should be included in local plans
Comparison of service patterns and practices
• The NSF promises to develop a system of benchmarking to monitor the use of services by older people
Engagement of staff
• The importance of involving staff in discussions about older people's services and of offering adequate support and training to meet older people's needs is clearly stated
• No explicit targets have been set

Appendix B

Survey letter sent to potential interviewees

Dear _____

Age discrimination in health and social care

As you may know, the Government recently published a new *National Service Framework for Older People* which aims to improve health and social services for older people by 'rooting out age discrimination' and promoting health and independence. The King's Fund has, for some time, been aware of discriminatory policy and practice in the NHS and in social services and we would now like to do what we can to help colleagues responsible for local services as they implement this latest NSF.

We plan to establish a development programme to support people providing local services. However, we would like first of all to hear what senior managers think about the opportunities and problems they expect to face regarding age discrimination in health and social care.

I am writing to ask whether you would be willing to take part in consultations we plan to hold with senior managers in different parts of the NHS and social services. These consultations are intended to seek your views about services provided for older people in your area, and to hear about any ideas or concerns you may have about implementing action on age discrimination. We shall also be keen to hear about any recent developments in your area that you think may help to combat age discrimination.

Consultations will be conducted through telephone interviews which should take no longer than 20-30 minutes. The interviews will be conducted by King's Fund staff: Emilie Roberts and Linda Seymour. All interviews will, of course, be confidential and no individual or organisation will be identified in any report.

Information gathered through these consultations will be used to inform the development programme mentioned above. This is intended to help health and social care organisations as they implement the *NSF for Older People* by advising on effective action, and promoting innovative and good practice developments from around the country.

I do hope you will agree to take part in this preliminary phase of the programme. Naturally, we will provide you with feedback from the consultations, and will send you a summary of the key messages arising from our interviews with senior managers.

Emilie Roberts or Linda Seymour will be calling your office in the next week or so to ask whether you are willing or able to help, and, if so, to book a date and time for the telephone interview. In the meantime, if you require any further information, please contact Janice Robinson, Director of Health and Social Care at the King's Fund.

Yours sincerely

Rabbi Julia Neuberger
Chief Executive
Programme

Janice Robinson
Director of Health and Social Care

Appendix C

Telephone interview schedule on age discrimination

Name _____

Position _____

Organisation _____

Date of interview _____

Record of contacts made

If non-responder, record any reason given for not participating here

---

Introduction

Check if received letter and ask if willing to take part.

If unwilling,

- Repeat that confidential and no individual person or organisation will be identifiable in any report
- Echo aims of the consultation in letter, for example:

Could say that want to get an accurate picture of how age discrimination is perceived by senior managers so that future work on this issue is constructive and relevant, and moves on from simply stating that it exists or doesn't.

- If respondent cites workload/ignorance of issues as factor for not taking part busy, ask if they could nominate someone else that we could approach in their place

---

Context

1. Can you briefly describe the services that .... provides?
(name organisation)

If talking to a different respondent to that named on the original sample list and their job/role is not clear then also ask:

2. Can you briefly describe your role in the organisation?

Interviewer notes
Interested in thumbnail sketch of all services/responsibilities not just those relating to older people

Age discrimination

3. Now, thinking about age discrimination, as a manager, have you been aware of age discrimination in the services you are responsible for?

If yes, prompt along the following lines (unless already covered in earlier response)

3.1 Do you think this type of discrimination is sporadic or systematic in nature?

3.2 Why do you think age discrimination has occurred on these occasions?

Interviewer notes
If specific instances of discrimination are described, try and probe for source of evidence, e.g. complaints, explicit policy, or personal observation.

Access to services

If respondent employed by PCT/G, ask
4. Is access to primary and community health services in your area ever directly related to a patient's age?

If respondent employed by community or acute trust, ask
4. Is access to your Trust's services ever directly related to a patient's age?

If respondent employed by social services department, ask
4. Is access to social services in your area ever directly related to a client's age?

If no, prompt as follows

For respondents in social services departments
4.1 For example, in many areas, there are different cost ceilings on packages of care for older people compared to other groups

For respondents in community trusts, PCG/Ts
4.1 For example, in some areas there are age-based criteria for chiropody services

If yes, then ask

4.2 Of course, age-based criteria may be justified – do you think that they are reasonable in this case?

Quality of care

5. First, thinking about the physical environment, buildings and facilities

If respondent employed by PCT/G, ask
Do you think there is any difference in the quality of primary and community services provided to older people compared to younger patients?

If respondent employed by community or acute trust ask
Do you think there is any difference in the quality of care that the trust provides to older people compared to younger patients?

If respondent employed by social services department, ask
Do you think there is any difference in the quality of social care services provided to older people compared to younger patients?

Note to interviewers
We're interested in any observable differences even if work to older people's advantage rather than disadvantage

6. Now thinking about staff skills and attitudes towards older people

If respondent employed by PCT/G, ask
Do you think there is any difference in the quality of primary and community services provided to older people compared to younger patients?

If respondent employed by community or acute trust, ask
Do you think there is any difference in the quality of care that the trust provides to older people compared to younger patients?

If respondent employed by social services department, ask
Do you think there is any difference in the quality of social care services provided to older people compared to younger patients?

Age discrimination as a priority issue

7. Has age discrimination been recognised or discussed at board or committee level in your organisation in the last year?

If yes, ask what prompted this?

- evidence of age discrimination in local services?
- priority-setting or other strategic planning?
- the *National Service Framework for Older People*?
- other factor

8. Do you think age discrimination is likely to be an issue raised at senior management level in the coming year?

Age discrimination can be quite subtle and hidden. It's not always easy to observe. So I want to ask some more general questions about older people's services. I want to stress that we're not looking for 'right' or 'wrong' answers here.

9. Would you say that older people's services are a priority in your trust/social services department/PCG (as appropriate)

Interviewer notes
If get a yes/no response, prompt for examples or evidence

Public involvement

10. In what ways are older people formally consulted about services?

11. Are 'harder to reach' older people targeted for consultation, for example, black elders, and older people with mental health or mobility problems?

12. Have older people themselves raised the issue of age discrimination?

Attractiveness of working in older people's services

If respondent is employed in a community trust, PCT or social services department, ask

13. In your current experience, is recruitment and retention of staff for older people's services more difficult than for other services?

OR, if respondent is employed in an acute trust, ask

13. In your current experience, is recruitment and retention of staff in specialties focusing on care of older patients more difficult than other specialties?

NB: don't ask this question to employees of PCGs

If yes, then ask

13.1 What do you think are the underlying reasons for recruitment and retention problems in these services?

Partnerships

14. How effectively would you say that local health and social care agencies work in partnership to meet the needs of older patients/clients? (as appropriate)

Would local services suit you?

15. Hypothetically, if you were an older person in ...., would you have confidence in local services to meet your health and social care needs effectively? (state geographical area)

Tackling age discrimination

16. We are really keen to find out what is being done to tackle age discrimination locally. Are you aware of any action or development that will tackle ageism or age-discrimination in your trust/local area at the moment?

17. Has your organisation attempted to do any of the following:

Tick if yes, and note details below

- Training for staff on ageing or older people's needs
- Inclusion of age in any equality and diversity strategy
- Designate senior managers/non executives or councillors* *(if social services)* as older people's champions or leads for older people's services
- Explicit policy statements/goals on age discrimination
- Audit trust/social services age-related policies
- Attract and retain older members of staff in your workforce, for example through a flexible retirement policy

18. Finally, do you think there could be any adverse consequences of highlighting age discrimination as an explicit issue that needs to be tackled in the *National Service Framework for Older People*?

Thank you very much for your time. We will send you a summary of the results later in the summer.

Appendix D

Characteristics of the interviewees in the survey

Organisation	Initial approach	Response rate (%)	Completed interviews (%)		
			Delegated	Male	Female
Primary care trust/group	Chief executive	21 (84%)	13 (17%)	7 (9%)	14 (19%)
Community NHS trust	Chief executive	21 (84%)	12 (16%)	8 (11%)	13 (17%)
Acute NHS trust	Medical director	11 (44%)	3 (4%)	8 (11%)	3 (4%)
Social services dept	Director	22 (88%)	11 (15%)	15 (20%)	7 (9%)
Total			39 (52%)	38 (51%)	37 (49%)

Appendix E

Specific examples of discriminatory service provision identified at the time of the survey

Patient group	Service	Discrimination
Older people	Hospital redeveloped with dedicated wards and staff for elderly. All people aged over 75 and younger patients with multiple pathologies	Direct
Black and minority ethnic older people	Some ethnic minority groups at high risk of heart disease have the lowest rate of access to coronary artery bypass graft	Unclear
Older people	Mental health services (several respondents)	Both
Older people	Health visitors focus on the under fives age group (two respondents). District nurses are struggling to manage 'huge' caseloads including 'high tech' work and palliative care	Both
Older people	In the coronary heart disease programme sometimes (older) people get 'stuck' and don't receive the best care	Direct
Older people	Physical disability unit for younger adults up to age 65; under review	Direct
Older people	Rehabilitation and intermediate care for people up to 65 years	Direct
Older people	Older patients labelled as 'bed-blockers' or 'acopia' (i.e. social admission) suffering from septicaemia and bone fracture	Direct
Older people	Range and scope of services for older people limited compared with other client groups, e.g. domestic cleaning services not available to older people	Direct
Older people	Some GPs treat older patients in a way that younger patients would not tolerate, e.g. an older patient denied treatment in one surgery because their notes were held in a different location	Direct
Older people	Specialist neuro-rehabilitation services focuses on return to work and so have an age restriction of up to 65 years (several respondents in different areas)	Direct
Older people	Stroke team had age criteria because of volume of demand; recently extended up to age 75	Direct

Patient group	Service	Discrimination
Older people	The patient's GP decides whether a general or elderly specialist is required upon hospital admission	Direct
Older people	Waiting times for cataract surgery	Indirect
Older people	Insufficient funding to provide Aricept to Alzheimer's disease sufferers in line with National Institute for Clinical Excellence (NICE) guidelines	Indirect
Older people	Some nursing home residents have poorer access to primary care services	Indirect
Older people	Variable admission routes or care pathways for stroke (two respondents)	Indirect
Older people	Aids and equipment: 'massive areas of discrimination' (several respondents)	Indirect
Younger people	Access to hearing aids	Direct
Younger people	Some of the community hospitals do not take people under 65	Direct
Younger people	Access to rehabilitation and recuperation services limited for people under 60	Direct
Younger people	Chiropody: priority given to older people (several respondents)	Direct
Younger people	Intermediate care and re-ablement service: priority given to older people	Direct
Younger people	Rapid response team limited to people over 65; however, age bar likely to be removed	Direct
No clear view	Care of elderly wards admit people over 77 (two respondents in area)	Direct